A Picture Book of Sitting Bull

David A. Adler

illustrated by Samuel Byrd

Holiday House / New York

Library of Congress Cataloging-in-Publication Data
Adler, David A.
A picture book of Sitting Bull / by David A. Adler ; illustrated by Samuel Byrd. — 1st ed.
p.   cm.
Summary: A brief biography of the Sioux chief who worked to maintain the rights of Native American people
and who led the defeat of General Custer at the Little Big Horn in 1876.
ISBN 0-8234-1044-7
1. Sitting Bull, 1834?–1890—Juvenile literature.   2. Dakota Indians—Juvenile literature.
3. Hunkpapa Indians—Biography—Juvenile literature.   [1. Sitting Bull, 1834?–1890.
2. Dakota Indians—Biography.   3. Indians of North America—Great Plains—Biography.]
I. Byrd, Samuel, ill.   II. Title.
E99.D1S5615   1993   92-47119   CIP   AC
978'.004975'0092—dc20
[B]

Other books in David A. Adler's *Picture Book Biography* series

A Picture Book of George Washington
A Picture Book of Abraham Lincoln
A Picture Book of Martin Luther King, Jr.
A Picture Book of Thomas Jefferson
A Picture Book of Benjamin Franklin
A Picture Book of Helen Keller
A Picture Book of Eleanor Roosevelt
A Picture Book of Christopher Columbus
A Picture Book of John F. Kennedy
A Picture Book of Simón Bolívar
A Picture Book of Harriet Tubman
A Picture Book of Florence Nightingale
A Picture Book of Jesse Owens
A Picture Book of Anne Frank
A Picture Book of Frederick Douglass
A Picture Book of Rosa Parks

Sitting Bull was a Native American, part of the Hunkpapa, one of seven bands of the Western Sioux tribe. He was born in March 1831 on the bank of the Grand River in what is now South Dakota.

When Sitting Bull was young, huge herds of buffalo roamed across the Great Plains. The Sioux ate buffalo meat and used the hides to make bedding, robes, and tepees. They made spoons and cups from buffalo horns and ropes and belts from the animal's hair. They wasted nothing and killed only as many buffalo as they needed to survive. Sitting Bull killed his first buffalo when he was ten years old.

Women tanning buffalo hides.

Sitting Bull was first named Slow because he never seemed to be in a hurry. His father, Returns-Again, and his mother, Mixed-Days, also had two daughters. Slow was their only son.

When he was fourteen, Slow fought his first battle against his tribe's enemies, the Crow. He put on war paint and rode out to join the older Sioux warriors. He carried a *coup*-stick, a long straight stick with a feather on one end. It was considered an act of bravery to touch the enemy with it, to "count coup."

When Slow saw one of the enemy, he rode quickly ahead. He hit the Crow warrior and knocked the bow and arrow from his hand.

After winning the battle, the Sioux warriors went home. Returns-Again described how his son had counted coup. Then he announced, "My son is brave. I name him *Tatanka Iyotake*, Sitting Bull."

That name had special meaning for Returns-Again. Several years earlier, he told of a giant buffalo that had walked toward him muttering, "Sitting Bull, Jumping Bull, Bull With Cow, Bull All Alone." Returns-Again believed those names were a gift from the Buffalo God.

At first he took the name Sitting Bull for himself. But after his son had shown such bravery, he gave him that name and changed his own to Jumping Bull.

Several years later Sitting Bull married. His first wife was named Scarlet Woman. They had a son, but the winter after the boy was born was so cold that both Scarlet Woman and the baby died.

It was common for Hunkpapa Sioux men to have several wives, often more than one at a time. After Scarlet Woman died, Sitting Bull had many wives and many children.

Sitting Bull with two of his wives and children.

Sitting Bull spoke of events that would happen in the future. When some of his predictions came true, he became known among his people as a medicine man and prophet.

As a young man, Sitting Bull fought his greatest battles against Native American enemies. When he was older, he fought against white settlers and soldiers of the United States government.

At first, the only white men Sitting Bull saw were traders. But beginning in the 1840s, many pioneers went west. They traveled through Sioux land and built houses, towns, and forts. They also killed millions of buffalo for their hides and for sport. By the 1880s, the great herds of buffalo would be gone, and along with them, the way of life of the Plains Native Americans.

There were many battles. Sitting Bull hated the ways of the white men. He called on his people to chase them off Native American land. Peace treaties with the United States government and Native Americans were written, signed, and broken by white men.

In November 1868 another treaty was written. In exchange for peace, the Sioux would keep some territory and give up some to the government. The land they kept would form The Great Sioux Reservation. The treaty was signed by many Sioux leaders, but not by Sitting Bull.

He was a proud man. He loved his people and their way of life. "I will not have my people robbed," Sitting Bull said. He would not agree to giving up any part of Sioux land, and he refused to live on the reservation.

Soon after the treaty was signed, it was broken. Hundreds of white prospectors came to search for gold on the reservation in the sacred Black Hills.

On December 22, 1875 Sitting Bull learned that the United States government ordered all Native Americans to move onto the reservations by the end of January. Those who didn't move would be considered a threat to peace and "would be treated accordingly by the military force."

The government order was an impossible one to obey. December 1875 was the beginning of a very cold, severe winter. Great snow drifts covered the more than two hundred miles between the Powder River, where Sitting Bull was camped, and the reservation.

Sitting Bull said, "They want war. All right, we'll give it to them!"

In the spring thousands of Native Americans from other tribes joined Sitting Bull and his Sioux warriors. Sitting Bull told them, "We must stand together" or they will kill us all one at a time.

Sitting Bull did a Sun Dance, a religious ceremony. Sticks were pushed through his skin and tied to a center pole. He danced for two days without food or water until he collapsed and had a vision.

He saw soldiers on horseback with their heads down and their hats flying off, falling from the sky like grasshoppers. It was a message to Sitting Bull from Wakan Tanka, the Great Spirit. The Native Americans would have a great victory.

Sitting Bull warned his people not to look for any profit from the fight. "Do not take their guns or horses . . . If you set your hearts upon the goods of the white man, it will prove a curse to this nation."

On June 25, 1876, at Little Bighorn River, Montana, the Native Americans killed Lieutenant Colonel George Armstrong Custer and the more than two hundred soldiers he led. This fight became known as the Battle of the Little Bighorn and ''Custer's Last Stand.'' It was the Sioux's last great victory.

In the months that followed, soldiers chased after the Sioux, burned their camps, and killed their families. Their reservation was made smaller. Some of the land promised to the Sioux for "as long as the grass shall grown and the waters shall flow," including the Black Hills, was taken away.

In February 1877 Sitting Bull led the Hunkpapa Sioux north, into Canada.

It was peaceful there, but buffalo were scarce. The winter of 1881 was harsh, and the Hunkpapa had little to eat. In July 1881 Sitting Bull and his people, starving and weak, returned to the United States.

Sitting Bull was arrested and held prisoner in Fort Buford and Fort Randall until 1883. Then he was forced to live on the reservation.

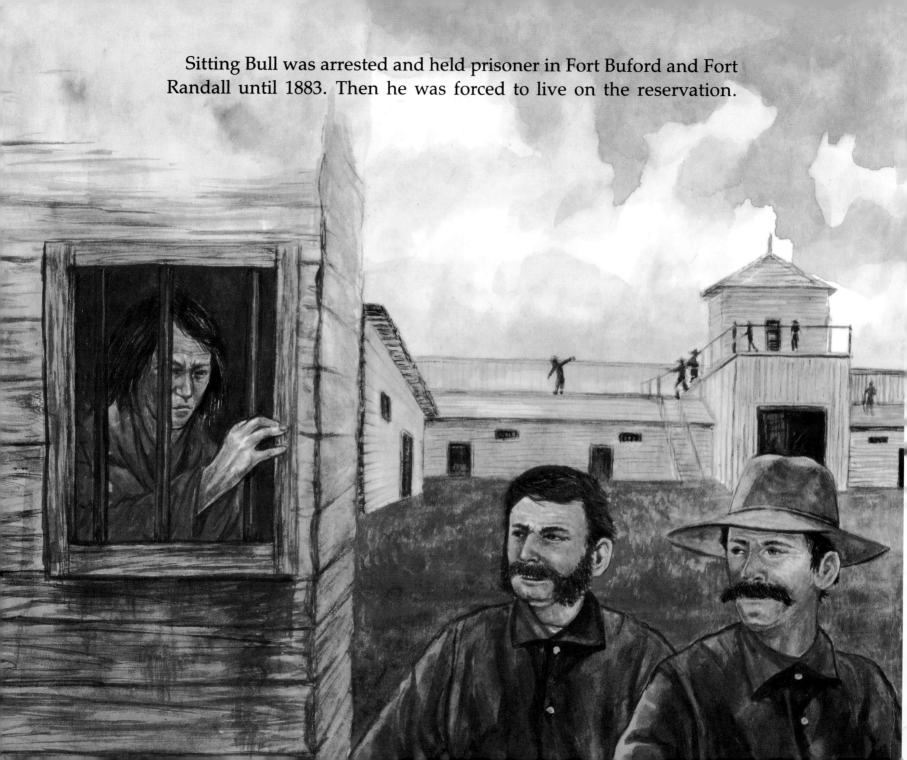

In 1885 Sitting Bull joined Buffalo Bill Cody and Annie Oakley in their Wild West Show.

They went on a tour of cities in the East. Thousands of people came to see Sitting Bull. They crowded around him to get his autograph. He gave most of the money he earned to poor beggar children.

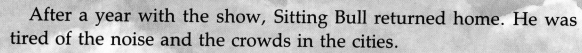

After a year with the show, Sitting Bull returned home. He was tired of the noise and the crowds in the cities.

In 1889, the government broke the Treaty of 1868 again. The Sioux were forced to sell much of their land to white settlers.

These were hard times for Native Americans. There was little rain or food on the reservations and much disease.

Then, in 1890, Wovoka, a Paiute Native American, told his people they could bring back their dead by doing the Ghost Dance. It would also bring great herds of buffalo and floods which would drown their white enemies. Sitting Bull did not believe the dance could bring back the dead, but he felt the dance might bring his people hope.

Soon thousands of Sioux were dancing wildly. Government agents were sure it was a war dance. They were frightened. If there would be war, they were sure that Sitting Bull would lead it. They arrested him on December 15, 1890.

A crowd of Sitting Bull's friends and family gathered.

"I am not going!" Sitting Bull cried out.

There was a riot. Sitting Bull's son, Crow Foot, was dragged out from under a bed and killed. Others were killed, too, including Sitting Bull. Across the Plains, Native Americans mourned and danced the Ghost Dance.

Hundreds of Hunkpapa Sioux were frightened. They ran off and joined Sioux Chief Big Foot, but on December 29, 1890, they were trapped by soldiers at Wounded Knee Creek, South Dakota. More than two hundred mostly unarmed Sioux men, women, and children were shot. Black Elk, a Native American who witnessed the killings, wrote many years later that the dead "had never done any harm and were only trying to run away."

Sitting Bull was a brave man, proud to be a Native American. Perhaps he is best remembered by his own words. In 1890, shortly before he was killed, he said, "The red man's ways are best for the red man." And in 1882, before a committee of United States senators, he said of himself, "My heart is red and sweet."

IMPORTANT DATES

1831	Born in March on the bank of the Grand River.
1841	Killed his first buffalo.
1845	Name changed to Sitting Bull.
1864	United States soldiers under General Alfred Sully attacked and burned the Hunkpapa camp.
1868	Treaty setting up The Great Sioux Reservation was signed.
1870s & 1880s	The last large herds of buffalo were killed.
1876	The Battle of Little Bighorn River was fought. The Seventh Cavalry, led by Lieutenant Colonel George Armstrong Custer, was defeated by a Native American force.
1877–1881	Lived in Canada.
1881	Arrested upon his return to the United States.
1883	Moved to the Sioux reservation.
1885	Joined Buffalo Bill Cody's Wild West Show.
1890	Killed on December 15.
1890	More than two hundred mostly unarmed Sioux were killed at Wounded Knee Creek, South Dakota, on December 29.

AUTHOR'S NOTE

Though he needed animals for food, Sitting Bull had great respect for them. Before he killed an animal, he whispered, "My children are hungry." And when he came upon the bones of dead bison, out of respect, he turned their skulls to face the sun.

The animal commonly called the American buffalo is called the *bison* by zoologists. Conservationists rallied to it and today the buffalo are no longer in danger of becoming extinct.

The United States government recognized Sitting Bull as a chief of the Hunkpapa Sioux, but to his own people he was a medicine man, a spiritual leader.

Some historians question whether Sitting Bull gave away money to beggar children while touring with Buffalo Bill's Wild West Show, but it is a well-accepted legend.

In 1492 Christopher Columbus thought he had reached the Indies and called the people he found there "Indians." But these people had lived in America long before Columbus came and are rightfully called Native Americans.

JUV/E
E
99
.D1
S5615
1993

$15.95

Adler, David A.

A picture book of
    Sitting Bull.

DATE			
AUG	1996		

BAKER & TAYLOR